Turtle, Turtle, Watch Out!

April Pulley Sayre

Illustrated by Annie Patterson

Charlesbridge

Late one night, on a beach in Florida, a baby turtle's story begins. It could be a short story—or no story at all—if not for helping hands.

Turtle is only an egg now. Her mother's flippers cover her with sand.

Hungry raccoons watch. And when Mother Turtle crawls
back to sea . . .
Furry feet scurry. Noses sniff. Paws dig.

Turtle, Turtle, watch out!

Young hands, holding a flashlight, scare the bandits away.

They place wire mesh around the turtle nest to protect the buried eggs.

Morning comes. So does a Jeep. It speeds toward the eggs.

Turtle, Turtle, watch out!

The Jeep stops. Hands have put up a painted sign.
NO DRIVING ON THE BEACH, the sign says.
The Jeep leaves. The turtle nest is safe and undisturbed.
Turtle sees none of this, inside her egg.

Two months later, Turtle begins to tear her leathery eggshell. She rips it open with a special tooth. She rocks and wiggles to escape. Then she rests, still half in her shell. Her yolk sac, attached to the bottom of her shell, shrinks as her body absorbs its energy.

A day later, nudging and pushing, she and the other hatchlings dig toward the surface. They scramble, then rest. Scramble, then rest. Their upward journey takes three whole days.

Finally, on a moonlit August night, Turtle peeks out of the sand. Other hatchlings below her are pushing her upward. All around her, the hatchlings dig out.

Pushing against the sand, Turtle crawls across the beach. Go to the light! That's all Turtle knows. At night the brightest light should be the horizon over the sea.

Tonight it is not. Turtle crawls toward the wrong light, shining from across the street.

Turtle, Turtle, watch out!

Small hands switch off the light. Turtle turns and crawls the other way. She scurries toward the ocean waves.

Step by step, she journeys down the beach. Animals gather: night herons, cats, and raccoons. They are hungry and are here to eat the hatchlings.

Turtle, Turtle, watch out!

Quickly, Turtle scoots to the water. *Whoosh!* Water picks her up and carries her seaward, then pushes her back toward the beach. *Whoosh!* Waves tumble her tiny body, then carry her to sea again. She pushes her flippers. She can swim! She swims past hungry fish. Currents catch her and carry her far from shore.

For months, she drifts in patches of seaweed. She dines on tiny plants and animals. She grows. Currents carry her thousands of miles, circling an ocean wide, until one day she leaves the floating sargassum, a mass of algae. She begins to swim. Past islands. Past sailfish. Past humpback whales.

She reaches a coral reef, where she spies a tasty jellyfish. . . .

Turtle, Turtle, watch out!

Splash! Quick hands dip down, grabbing the plastic bag.
It looks like a jellyfish, but it is not. It could choke a turtle
or clog its belly.

Turtle swims onward. She looks for other food. As she
grows, her jaws crack open conchs, crabs, and clams.
For twenty years this is her turtle life . . . until one day
she feels restless.

It is time for her to travel, far and fast. She flaps her
flippers like underwater wings. She swims and swims—
past ships, sailing and sunken.

Three sharks see her.

Turtle, Turtle, watch out!

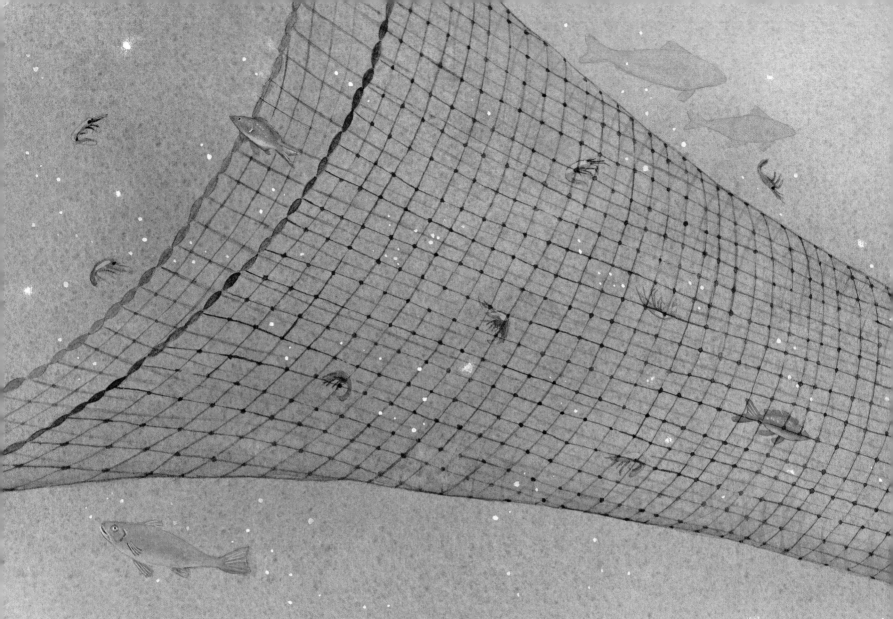

The sharks pursue her. No hands can help her now. She
swims faster and faster—and finally escapes! But she does
not see a shrimper's nets rushing toward her.

Turtle, Turtle, watch out!

In an instant she is swept into a net. It drags her down, down. She needs to surface to breathe. The boat pulls, tumbling her to the back of the net. She is almost out of air—when she slips through an escape hatch. She is free! Months before, weathered hands had sewn that hatch onto the net, just so sea turtles could escape.

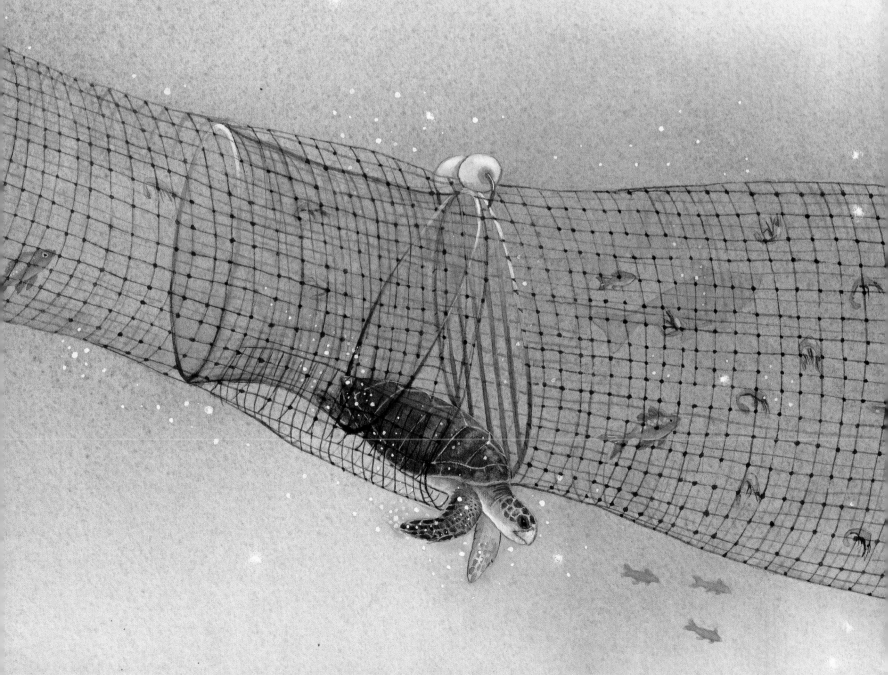

Shaken but safe, Turtle swims on. She meets a male turtle, and they mate. Later, under a summer moon, Turtle swims toward the breaking waves.

Thud! Her heavy body hits the hard shore. It is the same beach where she hatched. But now things are different: now she is a mother turtle, about to lay her eggs.

One day those eggs will hatch. The tiny turtles will begin their journeys, scrambling across the sand. And some will make it, with a little luck, and fast-moving flippers, and the help of many hands.

Helping Hands for Sea Turtles

All seven species of sea turtles are rare and in danger of extinction. So all over the world, people are helping them survive.

- In Costa Rica volunteers patrol beaches looking for sea turtle nests and protecting them from poachers—people who illegally steal the eggs.

- In Texas people clean trash off beaches so that mother turtles can more easily climb onshore and baby turtles can more easily scramble to sea.

- In Hawai'i volunteers stand guard to help keep rats, mongooses, pigs, and birds from eating hawksbill turtles rushing to sea.

- In Florida beachfront homeowners and renters join NESTS (Neighbors Ensuring Sea Turtle Survival). During hatching season they turn off lights near the beach to prevent young turtles from crawling in the wrong direction. Volunteers with state permits place wire mesh over sea turtle nests so raccoons cannot eat the eggs.

- In South Carolina kids work with state biologists to help hatching turtles climb out of deep vehicle tracks, where the tiny turtles can get stuck. Driving on some beaches is banned because vehicles can crush turtle nests.

- Off the coast of North Carolina, shrimpers are putting Turtle Excluder Devices (TEDs)—special escape hatches—on their nets so the turtles will not drown if they are caught in them.

- In India the government has launched Project Sea Turtle to help protect beaches and install TEDs on commercial fishing nets.

Even people who don't live near beaches are helping sea turtles.

- At home, families are reusing plastic bags and making sure their trash is properly disposed. That way their plastic bags won't end up on a beach or out at sea. (Sea turtles sometimes eat bags accidentally, thinking they are jellyfish.)

- People are also raising money to purchase coastal land so that beach areas can be set aside for sea turtles to nest undisturbed. Thanks to many donations, The Nature Conservancy and National Park Service bought and set aside Kamehame Beach in Hawai'i as a protected area for turtle nesting.

- Turtle activists are talking with government officials about passing laws that protect sea turtles. They are asking lawmakers not to allow oil drilling near beaches where turtles nest.

Helping hands in many lands are working for sea turtles every day!

To find out more about sea turtles, visit www.seaturtle.org.
For information on satellite tracking of turtles through the ocean, check
www.seaturtle.org/tracking.

To learn more about how you can help sea turtles, contact:
Caribbean Conservation Corporation
4424 NW 13th Street
Suite B-11
Gainesville, FL 32609
1-800-678-7853
email: ccc@cccturtle.org
Visit their sea turtle website at **www.cccturtle.org**.

Sea Turtle Species

Each of the seven species of sea turtle has a different life history and range. Most sea turtles do not begin nesting until they are at least twenty years old. In general, a female turtle nests every two to four years. During a nesting summer, the mother turtle may nest up to six or seven times, and each nest can contain one hundred eggs or more. The eggs hatch after fifty to sixty days, then the young hatchlings scramble to the sea. The IUCN (International Union for the Conservation of Nature) lists all except the flatback turtles of Australia as endangered or critically endangered.

Loggerhead turtle *(Caretta caretta)*

The loggerhead turtle, depicted in this book, is the main sea turtle species nesting along the eastern coast of the United States. Loggerheads also nest in Central and South America, the Mediterranean, Australia, and Japan. One of their major nesting sites is in Oman, a country in the Middle East. An adult loggerhead weighs about 350 pounds (159 kilograms)—as much as a refrigerator full of food! Loggerheads eat crabs, clams, sea snails, jellyfish, and other small sea creatures. Their large muscled heads control strong jaws that can crack open a heavy conch shell to get to the meat inside.

Green turtle *(Chelonia mydas)*

Green turtles swim in the Atlantic, Pacific, and Indian oceans and in the Caribbean Sea. An adult green turtle can weigh as much as 400 pounds (182 kilograms). Their name comes from their green fat, a result of all the sea grass and algae they eat. Green turtles' bodies are slightly larger than loggerhead turtles' bodies, but their heads are smaller. They have serrated beaks to help them cut vegetation. One of the major nesting sites for green turtles is at Tortuguero, Costa Rica. Another is Raine Island, Australia.

Leatherback turtle *(Dermochelys coriacea)*

The leatherback, the largest of all turtles, can be six feet (1.8 meters) long and can weigh over 1,500 pounds (680 kilograms). Instead of a shell, it is covered in thick, rubbery skin. Leatherbacks eat primarily jellyfish. Leatherbacks, now very rare, nest in small numbers in North America, South America, Africa, Asia, Australia, and the Caribbean.

Hawksbill turtle (*Eretmochelys imbricata*)

Hawksbill turtles weigh only around 150 pounds (68 kilograms). Their name comes from their hooked beak, which acts like a pair of clippers. They drift along reefs, snipping off and eating bits of natural sponges. Hawksbill turtles spend most of their time in coral reefs. They live in the warm waters of the tropics, such as the Caribbean Sea, coastal South America, the waters off northeast Australia, the Indian Ocean, and the Red Sea. A major reason this turtle is endangered is that its beautiful shell has been used for jewelry and other ornaments. International trade of hawksbill shell is now banned, which is helping turtle populations recover.

Kemp's ridley (*Lepidochelys kempii*)

The world's most endangered turtle, Kemp's ridley, weighs as much as one hundred pounds (45 kilograms). Most nest in Rancho Nuevo, Mexico, and a few nest in Texas. Dedicated conservationists in both places have gone to great lengths to help this species survive. In Mexico these turtles come ashore in the thousands and nest all at once, in events called *arribadas*. (In Spanish *arribada* means "arrival.") Young Kemp's ridleys travel far and wide and are sometimes found near the beaches of Long Island Sound and even in Europe.

Olive ridley (*Lepidochelys olivacea*)

The smallest and most common of all sea turtles, olive ridleys weigh only about ninety pounds (41 kilograms). These olive green turtles eat crabs, shrimp, clams, snails, jellyfish, and algae. They live in the tropical parts of the Pacific, Indian, and Atlantic oceans. Like Kemp's ridleys, olive ridleys gather in *arribadas*.

Flatback turtle (*Natator depressus*)

Flatback turtles weigh almost 200 pounds (91 kilograms). These turtles swim in the waters near Australia and Papua New Guinea. Flatback turtles spend a lot of time close to shore. They eat sea cucumbers, seaweed, jellyfish, and other small ocean creatures.

For Pearl and the Richardson Turtle Team—A. P. S.

For all sea turtles, and for all those who help them—A. P.

Acknowledgments: Thank you to Jeff Sayre for his sharp eyes that help find not only turtles but also manuscript issues. Thank you to Janice Blumenthal of the Cayman Islands Department of the Environment for her scientific review and for allowing us to participate in turtle research in the Cayman Islands. Our thanks also to Mark Orr.

First published in 2000 by Orchard Books.

Published by Charlesbridge
85 Main Street
Watertown, MA 02472
(617) 926-0329
www.charlesbridge.com

Library of Congress Cataloging-in-Publication Data
Sayre, April Pulley.
    Turtle, turtle, watch out! / by April Pulley Sayre ; illustrated by Annie Patterson.
        p. cm.
    Summary: From before the time she hatches until she returns to the same beach
to lay eggs of her own, a sea turtle is helped to escape from danger many times
by different human hands.
    ISBN 978-1-58089-148-6 (reinforced for library use)
    ISBN 978-1-58089-149-3 (softcover)
1. Sea turtles—Juvenile fiction. [1. Sea turtles—Fiction. 2. Turtles—Fiction.]
I. Patterson, Annie, 1975– ill. II. Title.
PZ10.3.S277Tu 2010
[E]—dc22   2008025338

Printed in China
(hc) 10 9 8 7 6 5 4 3 2 1
(sc) 10 9 8 7 6 5 4 3 2 1

Illustrations done in watercolor, gouache, and pastel on Arches paper
Display type set in Ogre, designed by Wayne Thompson, and text type set in Weiss
Color separations by Chroma Graphics, Singapore
Printed and bound September 2009 in Nansha, Guangdong, China
    by Everbest Printing Company, Ltd.
    through Four Colour Imports Ltd., Louisville, Kentucky
Production supervision by Brian G. Walker
Designed by Susan Mallory Sherman